pantry

ALSO BY LILAH HEGNAUER

Dark Under Kiganda Stars

pantry

LILAH HEGNAUER

poems

HUB CITY PRESS
SPARTANBURG, SC

First printing, February 2014
Book Design: Meg Reid
Printed in Saline, MI
by McNaughton & Gunn Inc.
Cover Photo © Kimberly Blok
Illustrations by Emily Caulfield

TEXT Garamond Pro 10.8 / 13.1
DISPLAY Garamond Pro 15

Library of Congress
Cataloging-in-Publication Data

Hegnauer, Lilah, 1982-
 [Poems. Selections]
 Pantry / Lilah Hegnauer.
     pages cm
 ISBN 978-1-938235-02-3 (paperback : alk. paper)
 I. Title.
 PS3608.E35A6 2014
 811'.6—dc23
        2013032678

186 West Main St.
Spartanburg, SC 29306
1.864.577.9349

for Anthony

CONTENTS

III.

IV.

V.

I

PIE BIRD

Was round again.
Was the reins and bridle

in hand, was saddled.
Was the fasten seatbelt sign is lit, was fooled.

Was curtsey & curdle, was anybody
home, was I their mother, was the heath

& gorse, this winter afternoon with driving
rain, my filly, my donkey, my mare.

Was cutting butter,
was tiny, one galosh, two ears, a hide

of pure tin. Wasn't far. Wasn't yours.
Was—why?—apple

or plum; was yours.
Was your left foot, was your crumb rubber

playground, was tire swing, was whisk
to your egg drop soup.

Was binding and glue and stitch, was
folio, was flacon, was fable.

BOWL

You were the sly, sly maiden unfingering her gloves.
You were the tallis, the quake, the narrows of the

sound, the birchbark. You were the bun,
you were the oven. You were festooned, a fistful,

the slow line at the market. You were the fur, the fox,
the too-small type, you made milk with your want,

you made wanting a full time job. You were the
upstairs neighbor with stilettos, the shuttered room

where, with peppery fits of exhaustion, you poured
me a second glass. You were the stopper and chain,

the bathwater, too. You were every last crumb,
you were licking the plate, you were still hungry.

PITCHER

It is your own lush self
you hunger for.
— Lucille Clifton

In the slack-shuttered camera, in hibiscus,
in Prussia, Cuba, Cuba, in a linen-covered
duvet which is based on the corners I covet:

me. Fraught with glibness, so the ginger
cats prance: imagine a neat, deep tub
and hot water that goes and goes. I

make it so. Imagine a stutter that stops
on L, L, L. Mine. Imagine that hot island
with a burr stuck in its trim hide.

Reader, how I thought I'd put a finger
through that thin, lit bubble
and become a better me. Of course

there was no bubble. Of course I'd stripped
to my skivvies in the middle of what
was just my own shower. And there, chilling

to a marrow-fine nerve, belonging to
my own wild head, fitting the width of my
big toe into the drain, I stood.

BURNING

I don't know how to woo you. Lightning
struck the city blind and I was its prophet seer.

I lost you then. And no river took us home.
And no roads lead home. And no market

to market, to buy a fat hog, and no home
again, home again, no jiggity jog. I've known

a heaven like a gate. And you were not its keeper.
I crept, a porter of your unknown hours.

Who you? Who, seriously, are you? A fawn.
A cobalt. A convalescent in a courtyard

in a time before mine. Whole milk scared you. You
cardiologist, you. What nothing undid you.

POEM

All I had to do was pull this thread and your stunt double came running, met me breathless at the corner, and said time me, I can fix this in 30 seconds flat. And he did. Who am I to say? He let the dog out with permission. That's not even his collar there.

We can say this of blasphemy: he was coercive. I didn't get time to wash my hair before he started in on me, calling my double blind, calling my hopeless bluffing, calling my selfsame colorist a thieving son of a gun. Only he didn't say gun.

He said I've got what you need/want. What was I supposed to do? Lean a ladder on his pony and steal his golden hen? I took him to bed right then and we put stays in our shirt collars in the morning and pretended fresh, pretended well rested and prepared and quiet evening at home.

PEAR

Cut quickly and nothing will spill.
(Everything spills tomorrow.)

I traffic in signs, hollow touch of rib to rib.
I don't remember much about my childhood

except my short legs and curly hair.
Incredulity and the thing that passes

for it. Help me but I like a love handle
after work, lounging on the couch,

shirt riding up. Yours could win prizes
at state fairs, blue ribbons at charity galas.

They could tango their way into movie premiers
and debutante balls. Baby humming

in the market stall, the hiss and thrum
of a brass hinge on an oak door.

ROLLING PIN

Novel heirlooms—lister, joist—
I could be wrong and glad.

Appallingly awkward, maybe I grasp
at everything. Our gathering, our coming

and going, burrowing our chestnuts
and nesting our scraps of twine:

maybe we will continue. Snow might
go on, despair might bring ease,

and I will believe something beyond
this body, this room, these cells you claim.

But if I'm right, and this failing,
heating, damned world and self

is our terminus, maybe I can know—
at least—infinity here. A piecrust so

flaky you could cry, an apple so small
and purple you could scalp it and dry it

for a mezuzah. The span of us only
this wide, on the verge of wrong.

SPOON REST

With thee, in the Desert—
With thee in the thirst—
　　　　　　—Emily Dickinson

Milkfish in the laundered night,
　　swept bare, these boards, listel
and lather, rugs upended in the slim
　　antechamber—barrow of pine
split small, your parka and boots
　　still dripping on the bricks.
And you, inside: once, I felt
　　a joy that was as old as a two
knees knocking, as a woodstove
　　ticking hot, as its stovepipe
about to ignite. Once I entered
　　a room on fire to read. If it is time,
anchor your heart and pack it
　　in your impossible cavity, lung,
lung, ribs, and veins. And keep the
　　kettle hot for me, and limber up.

(THE WORLD IS MY) OYSTER

it is my every fucking thing. It's true, no one put me up to this. I lost my own faith myself. You convert, you faulty ruin, you ripped schism, you foe.

No loss. No skin off my back. My aunt once said wool with cables, a dozen, they're easy, you could learn them in an afternoon. I did.

I strummed my stung and swollen fingers upon your strings. I fled burning cities. I flew unseen coops and left the hasp and click of everything going shut.

Lasso the horses, shutter the peephole, bring the whaler, the baker, the candles and snaps. What is life for if not to want it, tin gods and all.

PASTA PIN

Will wonders never cease. Disbelieve
   everything life has taught you
until now: good fences make good

backstops, kimchi can be mild, poems
   are a dime a dozen, black cats
run the show. Wake all the sleeping

babies, watched pots love it, summer
   won't last long, heat lessens, patience
gets easier, love is only a kind word

away. With your eyes and your mouth
   open—this is how you beckon true
love's kiss, every time, and if it's only

a fly that comes to bless you, swallow
   it and chase it with a spider. By the time you've
swallowed a cat, you'll meet a wealthy

otolaryngologist who will pull true love's
   kiss right out of you—mouth open and all.
See? The world is yours, entirely.

FLOUR SACK

We love the eve of holy days at home. We lose our mittens,
our heavy boots, toss the briefcases, unlace our braids,

and we, who were only ever employed tenuously to begin with,
throw off the mantle of this recession. We drink gin and we sing.

And you, young, blond curls limp in the heat, take karaoke requests
and queue them up and we all pretend, for a holy

day or two, that we have it all: enameled tubs, spoke and spoon
and spittle of all we won't actually say. You are more wanted

in this world than anything since or after. You are wanted like
a hasp wants its pin, like a comma wants another clause. Give it.

LINEN

Early September, & I'm gone for
miles this morning—all over nowhere, you say.

Above, branches of red birch,
my mind all sand & ended thoughts.

You stay. Teas in their jars, clasps
hinged tight, my hands, cut vines,

green thumbed catalogues.
We place orders, dream of potatoes,

red bliss and bison, celery, and thyme.
My mind might be nowhere—a sparse

thicket spinning, flotsam of evening,
but it's strung to yours.

TRIVET

I can turn boggy in the minstrel heat. I can
coppice and counter.

       I can grow coarse and sweaty
as elves, asking for nothing but you.

Haggard, good time, hubris, defiant for an anchor or
tide or shoal.

A record, only, of this: foamy stockpot, you
       could have been an ocean, for all I knew.

I live to want the lush and slippery world.
       I believe everything.

One day I will have a story for all this:
noon, leaves, day and chill

       and time and no you were not yet.
I knew there was you, I knew

your legs and beard and pearly snaps.
One day I will tell you

       how I burned and wanted to.

II

FRENCH PRESS

That I will know your body within mine.
That you will remain a stranger to me, still.

These are givens. That I will make you a lunch within a lunch.
Our bodies fooled and cavernous, I will take your

curly forelock and print it for stationery: boy! here! seven
pounds of boy. To keep from the butter dish, I will print

all of you, even the skeptic, even your tight jaw, even your
bald spot, your lip deceived by moustache, your other

lip stranded, your slim city all found out. I have been
clean. Silt. Vein. Ticker of tape. Quiet amid ruin.

DISHWASHER

Mortised twins, unlevered to the licked-clean cabinet,
who foretold your fortune? Me. Under it all,

I knew your thin fingers and latched buckles would
give. I knew the impossible heft of soapy water

and a full sink and a scrub brush. I knew appetite
and lank curls and breakfast waiting. I knew you.

LADLE

What came before
this fondant, boreal,

these housed, orectic
filaments—valid, sweaty,

needlessly flannel-
mouthed and punctual,

and affixed—but him:
swift little orecchiette

on the cutting board,
tenderizing the abalone,

parentheses, pistillate:
spoon, fever, & shell.

REAMER

This world will certainly extinguish.
Warmth fades, banked snow recedes

and rises. You slowly shovel a walk—
fret your beard with your teeth.

It keeps snowing.

Listen anyway.
All the time there is,
and very little to make of it.

Was there ever summer?
A great twilight moth
striking against your body—

I extinguish it all, I am certain.
All grasstops and the stilled wind,

every loosened rope ripens in
idle heat. And I shore this world with you.

POULTRY SHEARS

It might be possible to say these things
out loud with your socks
laddering at the toe, toe fossicking about.

First I watched you. Then I loved you.
I watched you again.

After I pulled the shive, wine ran
the sheaved wheels.

        Attics of red lit like brush.

And now I am full of wanting you
and having you, of the notched hook, we are.

By what authority but desire
can anyone say these things:

I would bring you X from the un-shimmed world.
I would trim plinths for your oceanic crust.

All the archetypes in tow, I would hoist
the febrile earth to my hip and chill it.

CANARY

We were writing, my erica, in darkness,
a darkening room, the last light, overdressed

for late spring. I fell asleep gazing at forget-
me-nots and dreamt of fight-me-nots, protect-

me-won'ts. I dreamt of flowers that tell the truth.
Chokecherry. Climbing lily. Bridal veil broom.

Woke remembering love-in-a-mist. Bleeding
heart. Love-lies-bleeding. Ladyfinger. Heartstring.

Remember glory-of-snow and glory-of-sun?
I want more. Safety-while-kissing, home-hard-won.

Obsession-with-red, flame bush, freckle face.
Marguerite, I want our world caught mid-race,

poppy off guard, like reading in a dark room,
these flower names: sweet cicely abloom

with summer holly, sweet william and sultan.
Stoneface only in poker, jasmine and royal ann

everywhere you look. Carissa and busy lizzie
and the fat morning glory in dishabille

of course, we wouldn't have it any other way.
I'll be your bachelor's button, I'll be your gay-

feather. I'll plant heather up our walk, and this
dahlia will swell, my hoop pine, my melissa.

We were writing, my plaid cactus, in the scrawny
shade of an old rosa. We weren't inside, bonnie,

we slept in the mattress vine all night, dreamt of
woolly blue curls potting and watering our dozen

lady slippers. We forgot the bearded iris.
We let the dame's rocket fly. We blew the thistle.

SINGING IT

Gust, suck the curtains out the window. I want you standing in a hot shower with an apple brandy perched on the edge of the tub.

Two stories up and three doors down, between my palms, feet hip-width apart and no one counting the breaths. I want a new tattoo, a fresh shake of salt, a few too many cooks in the kitchen. I want all my eggs in your basket. I move within a syllable of time and you, you watch me do it.

Snowpack and dewpond and kitties in the cupboard. Your clean clipped fingernails, your indecision, your hard to get, your grapefruit syrup weeping in unspooled threads, your darkroom door flung open.

DOUBLE BOILER

I'm known for my salt horse sandwiches.
He's known for his perfectly pithed
citrus. And together we're known

around this town for chocolate
soufflé. When it falls, he fills it with
what you will, berries, lemon curd,

mint cream, &c. I dust it with sugar
and leave it at your door. I pin
wheels in your garden. I mew hello

to your cat and scratch her arching
spine. There is no dinner but the one
we set about, flanged, flaming, late.

EGG TOPPER

And who's to stop us? The twin cities of barrel
and pepperbox? You are the Aegean to my Marmara;

in you, seas burn for names. In you, a little elbow
noodle wants for a plain, narrow cupboard.

We have it all. And then some. And the plainest
thing is this: marry me. Port arms! Time, and the

eye of a needle, metaphor, metaphor. As a pelt,
wrap it, cinch it, belt it, praise its luster.

CLEAVER

I caved; I hid. I stashed my groceries in your root cellar.
Basement, basement, what might be. And grew there

an onion of improbable red. In the dark tide, in the groan,
in the groin, the dome of my mouth ached to say, however

hasty, *twinge, twinned, twinset, Twin Falls, twin-screw, twine, twig.*
As for smart women, as for undyed linen, as for the space

between my shoulder and yours, in a theater, at a late night
show, a forever-and-ever sound, a hood of quiet, a simmer.

TABLE CLOTH

Long-winded and with you, the kitchen swept
of all our New Year's feasting, and you, spot lit

in front of the sink. I am lucky. I think two a.m.
exists only to make me sleepy and to want you.

Of the sky shot through with that cannon moon,
of it existing too—home is only the anatomy of

a hand, all those jointed fingers like an earlier version
of the species. Don't let the hot water run out.

This house covets all. It delivers us into the strangest
morning of all: that we have everything and then some,

even as the world burns; two matchbox cars
pulled back, even as their springs dissolve.

PEPPER

I thought I saw how the story got told.
And I gave it everything.
　　　　　—Sarah Manguso

Love is a rusty fire escape and the city is rangy. People trot in circles, the dogs are at their heels and catching up. The same reason haircuts are exhilarating. All those curls on the floor, the headiness of that light toss. Hyperventilation in the black apron. Thick knuckled fingers around the pepper's heft and glow. How stasis, how want. How women count eternity in days. Say lover as in present. Now slink through the salmonberries. The rows pulse. The radishes upturn in the soil.

Love is a hen. Pecked clean of corn, her gate is my gate. A penny, an envelope, a bell, a whistle—you, all, the pier, the pond—we throw dimes to say perhaps, but we know already that at the bottom of the well we have only the very ground we left.

Love is an egg topped and open and ready to eat. Joy is a beef knuckle for stock. My two cent darling, what more could we want? Each other cowed, all our money sunk, and an early sun—full, hot, undoing the night's ripe plums. This one short life is all—so lay it on thick. Shake the pepper till the table is gritty and hot. Then lick.

RAMEKIN

His hips gave so little, I could not
even blink. And then a wedge, spine
slipping open, click. A kingdom:

in the larkspur, in the goosefoot
of the gooseberry jam; in schools of
monkfish, of hyssop; of quarter round,

of ham. Saltwort and stalwart and every
lit splint of this man goes seeking
my face exactly as it is. How can I be

so now: enough, festooned, salt
fingering even limes, even mint, even
vodka with dinner. Let it snow. We

dream—it is good we are dreaming—
let the salt pigs squeal, let us blow
torch, let the sugar sing. Blind, incautious.

MORTAR & PESTLE

Those tufted ears,
    latticed by a chain
of speckle and filament:

barn door, owl, kitchen
    window, ourselves. We pocked
time into a thousand

episodic dinners: cardamom
    and bee balm, vanilla—
here's to marking them

against a future blight,
    alba withering in the
side yard, barn gone stale,

and me: childminder, cake,
    nightjar, potato, potato,
suckle and spit, egg and tomato.

WHISK

Long might this sky be familiar, embodied, fossae
and palm, and cinched the apron as a spigot

to heat me, rinsing and drying the berries
I handle and mash. Long the bulb

of these wires itself was a handbook: stiff,
peaked, wet and dry. Unready, too, tightly

pleated, coveting the hidden fold; the kit
of mink, the stolid wheat, the air of wholly

unremarkable noons and their sandwiches,
clumsy, homely, arctic, mine. I am a

maiden oven; watch me torch meringues.
Long this calibration might nimble me yours.

III

JAR

for Bruce Hegnauer

Late August, almost
light: a fishnet,
    a crab pot,

a salmon head for bait,
my father makes
    of this passage

an ocean. Lost watch,
that we could know
    anything

beyond this. Certain
in the half darkness,
    near dawn cave,

yaw, tunnel of self,
under a hillside
    covered in brambles,

love. He who once fell
through the plaster
    of a new ceiling

is still the ground of me.

SAUCER

Mollycoddled and asking for it,
my only defense is this: when life

threw me for a loop, I made spiral-
shaped flannel cakes. When I was

pistol whipped, I wept for joy.
When the air was let out of my sails,

I sallied forth. I stumbled upon. I
took it over easy. I slept and slunk

and sped and sputtered *parent,*
child, milk thistle, Shabbos, Shabbos,

Shabbos. Whose fault was that?
At the listening post, I made

a life of categories, and I kept
to them. My own heart

is an oak trunk at the foot
of the bed of long-dead royalty.

Fealty *(of course)* keeps me there. You
(of course) with your amber shadow,

willful as a hen unhoused, stopper
the night and tow me, oxish, lit, yours.

THERE IS NO MYSTERY

to the rain: it rains every night, vital
to each tulip as it was to my lantern of a self,

belly down in the low-slung fulcrum
of shyness; obdurate and unwieldy and refusing

to say *yes, I know you.* Little body, I thought
I had a vice grip on reality and wouldn't let it go.

I believed I hardened against downpour,
caulked my weak seams. I believed

hurry and happenstance. I believed,
mostly, in rain. I mean this literally.

9 X 13 INCH BAKING DISH

for Lilah Hook

What are there but orebodies, constellate
    in the bowl of a grandmother's mind,
what are there but handles of dippers, big

and little, lost and null lasagne recipes,
    knucklebones in a void and a risk,
the child's taut laces pinching mud.

Pioneers—through time's cloistering
    halt, clockfaces stripped, all returning
to the ultima Thule. For you: sweetness.

What are there but aprons, popeyed
    lace trim, tittuping generations
cinching the bow, now gone, now still here.

IF THE MIND

ruled the body, I'd be the first to know. Snow fell,
pacifying rhythm. Undone, impossibly thin hipped,

winsome and toothsome and mine. Yours is not
a voice that carries, and you speak at all the wrong moments,

interjecting for effect, letting others carry on without you.
Winter of tea and bathtubs, all that should not be written.

Convincing myself of your mouth, though it doesn't harbor here,
though it refuses me. Time moves in different directions.

One toward decay, one toward preservation,
holing up and tightening the hatchways.

APRON

Tell me the story again,
         how you made another body

of your own and kept him well & here. Imagine: his
enormous leather mittens, still filled. Bucket crowded

with unwashed russet potatoes. Loss is a far cry
from utterly unhinged, just me and my lattice windows.

He is gone, and no one in the world can remember the things I remember.

Little north, I call it like it is: I'll bite you.
I didn't come here to make friends. I came

to set the elvers swimming.
Pole to common pole, I'll keep you out.

It is a month and its relinquish I am talking about,
muddied hem, salted boots, the sorrel foal who will

chimney into the slippery dawn.

ICE PICK

also for Lilah Hook

Yours, yours, yours. I held your fluted mind
and lied. The best of me, the cream & curve

of this, the compline & canto of that,
the best of me, the butterbean vine, did not

come visit you today. She sent this one
instead, who cannot stop crying, who,

whittled back by the smell of urine
and confusion, looks at you and cries.

The crossing is not wide. A shepherd's
staff, a flock of geese, a footbridge, a moment.

We watch the rain—it will stop—and know
(boundless, trawling) nothing about anything.

TEA STRAINER

New Year's Eve, 2009

The sky yawned open its basket of stars
and the moon glowed on, and the vespertine
bowls steamed up our glasses; it was and it wasn't
the woolen night I ushered into winter.
It wasn't mine; I usher nothing; I wish and wish and wish.

STOCKPOT

The edge is what I have,
    and temerity, and a cliché rising
in a half glass of wine; nothing

was truly a geography of anything;
    I had bad luck. I stole the moon
and a pedigree. I had a dearth of dilettantes

but loved my lover better: he lost all grip.
    Immersed in our dome of a life,
in what stuck to roundness, I grew flighty

and fitful for rain, trees upon trees
    hiding madronas. Now—I tell you this
in strictest confidence—I am a weed.

I will smother you. Did you know
    what you were getting into with me
when I was born, bushy-headed and screaming,

and grew into a solemn tincture of compulsion.

SPOON

Your longing is not more than you ever imagined.
It's barely there, pulsing in the grocery bag.

You are at home with the kettle heating and vodka chilling.
You're in thick socks and boxer briefs, you're soaking in the clawfoot.

You're blinkered to all others. We have no records and licenses,
but we have eggs and milk. We have a pencil sharpener and a note pad.

Greenwater: raining and snowing, who can tell, and you,
buckling up cross country skis, light fading as it rises,

cat on the radiator, ice in the freezer. After you came home,
I stood and was calm, but I heated and heated and heated.

This story is not new. I've lived with my fist gripped
around my heart for years, saying *Quiet, you; you are not mine.*

EVERYTHING

Nothing of the world will sound outside of me,
low-toned and holding,

wringing your strings and scythes. Not one vent will blow.
No mothers will fill their sturdy shoes

and you were never enough.
Basil and spinach draining in the wire colander,

chatty as the sunburned throats
of artichokes.

If I put one leg around you in the night, if I press
your hands above your head—

have you ever seen such want?
You thought every last quarter and washer was mine.

My lemon tree, my soft spoken, unsayable—
why look at the want you carved out in me?

Till the chaste and manic soil.
Talk *it* back into silence.

SKILLET

Rally, joy, here. Weep here.
I am not lettered. I ferry
an even raft across your

pantry shelves: jimberry, jamberry,
red beans and black. Lentils
and popcorn and everything

you lack. I could pace your
acres and come to nothing—
still. No roots, no vines, no

frame, no sill. Consigned to a
pointy-ribbed filly, I address
you thus: rally here. I stocked
my shelves for you.

THEN

there was no body but a
jam jar upended on a drainboard.
Then there was no jam jar but its light refracted.
Then there was no light but two old dimes.
Then just a map, then just its monsters, then just their final spikes.

Then all were silent, and all thought *Noon. Hit me.*

Then a pocket, then a knife, then a pen
and a condom. Then a walk. These, our feet,
are built like barges. Tight little pilots could
land their bombers on our soles. Cover me.

Then there was no body but a

festival for beets and party pants. Then just
the brides and mothers. Then just ourselves,
and just our hatpins and just merriment and
time carved out of some chance walnut for a corridor.

IT'S ALL

gelid torpor and a lab rat on ecstasy. A full three months gone by
and still no word from the warden.

Irascible freedom and the heartburn
that comes too.

Modifiers, I'm done with you: milk stout,
a case full, these lollipops of grandeur

popping the question over and over:
how many licks does it take to get to—

Obedience, sultry lovechild, rescind your hold
on me. I want personality,

and I want it now.
I'm not your schoolmarm.

I'm not your run of the mill.
I'll drive a wedge,

a hard bargain, between your selves; I'll light a fire
under your seat. In terms of the consumption of wine,

we had our fill, our cups runneth, our heat off, our fire lit,
our master class in bells and whistles.

VASE

What eternal fest and show. Sugar on icing on cakes in July for weddings.
My oven. Absolute in my fortitude, I sought to herd you under the balcony stairs

and make of you a flame, errant and mine. Peonies arcing their pink bellies
above me, dahlias in the side yard, tight-lipped heliotrope snug to the bamboo.

I dreamed we were undressed and manic.
You lit the pilot and I tossed the greens and you threw the leeks

into a hot skillet and watched them hiss. Vinegar and olives and pasta and cheese.
What else could we want but wine? Chocolate. A table. Al Green on the radio

makes us puddle and kiss and skip sleep and monopolize the angry, worn out
good time of it all. Pulse of the unbegotten, we were enough, over and over.

IV

SIEVE

Tell me where—in what pestled vetiver
kitchen do you think you can set me quaking

with my
books sprung open, pages pinned

with jars of pie weights and peaches
and the washbasin full of thawing scallops

which I'll toss directly into the brown butter
thyme, into the improbable fevered

copper-bottomed expanse of our home. What
venous insufficiency, what plasterwork

cell, what pantryman's icebox, what bundle
of letters hidden between joists

in the ceiling of the Copland cabin
where on very cold nights a woman

listens to the fireplace tiles hiss and gasp
and hum. What stair, threshold, what

goatsucker, what hand in glove, what root cellar
housing a winterful of beets, turnips,

onions, what tasting spoon on the
sideboard in our kitchen, where we've

crushed the tomatoes and simmered
the cream and pinched the saffron

and roasted the fennel and let it meld,
where we took off our clothes

in the velvet dim of four PM in January
and had sex on the paisley armchair

and then cut the pasta that we boiled,
drained, sauced, and ate, and then licked up.

BREADKNIFE

for Herman Asarnow

I want only your nerves in my endings.

And a hearth. Keep me

on the lookout for noon, unimaginably awkward and here.

If you have this streak of indigent loneliness, I don't know it.

If you have a motto, it's *plenty*.

If you were a woman, you would be

decked out in gaiters, up to your knees in the snow
too short for this life

and loving it. I was only ready for the
momentous embers.

Hello mousseline frost and hassocks,

hello shuttered garden, rabbit warrens timorous
under the solstice field.

Here I am tending this fire in ignorance: all I know
is how to set it hissing.

REFUSAL

let me make a thing of cream and stars that becomes,
you know the story, simply heaven.
—Richard Siken

The hinge, its hidden polish,
the orange rind—take it,

I'll chew it.
Take the argument.
You'll always win.

I'll always tell myself
I let you.

All the gypsum,
all the kiln-glow of cobalt,

flares against my joy.
Let's be enough.

Take the documents.
I've seen egg whites
whipped for a tart.

You know what I mean.

FEAST

No night could drink enough, & no one ever said
we were rich with words.

Come to my cabin, come with your ink dry
and trunk full of wine. We'll swim in the still-warm passage

and grow itchy for Virginia: it all.
Yes, —, on evenings like this

I am stirred. But not for long.
Nothing in me houses you now, understand.

Emptied, I have every reason to want you. I love within the smallest
syllable, and you hesitate over even that,

dry skillet of each firethorn.
Before my eyes: hail and no downpour,

rice and no wedding, no berries
in chocolate

no warmth in the blue kettle I've left;
only this, which no words lift.

PASTRY BRUSH

I am ignitable. Strike a match and see
my lifetimes burn. This is the spun world,
wound up thick as cotton candy. Tidy
fears bolster and the malachite mountains
do bow low. Whatever we make of its rigs,
its flotillas, its fog through the parkway,
whatever we might claim as certain, I tell
you it will fill your copper pots and then some.

TEAPOT

I'll say it again: copper. I am a false smith of this metal, a worker of words, I say toolshed, say plated, say ache, but I let the obsession stand: copper this, copper that.

I know the pepper-scatter birds, out, around, and back again. I know how deep my impatience runs. I know measure and pour and stir. I know the mastery of want & its ungovernable root, like a field of snow, pocked, now, with wild onion.

Some mornings I am capable of that pure nothingness: I am nobody's milk tooth, nobody's rocky garden, no door, no mouse, no hive. But most mornings I am it all, brindle bruise, footsore & famishing.

CARAFE

Tomorrow adores me, smaller than a bee box. Smaller
than a bee's hind leg. Other things that adore me:

a melon rind, a mug, a pillow, a pair of linen
sheets. A quart of cider. Laundromat, butcher—

flattened out by love, Wednesday evening, cider.
Bend the track a little tighter, hop

the slow train into the elbow of what we can't see.
What is a heart in port? A foot, a toe, a goddamn leg.

I wait inside tomorrow, in a green skirt, on a page,
neatly folding the days, September, October.

CHURCHKEY

Here we are, infinity. What novel, thumbworn
decades have led exactly here: dwarves in their

heirloom bloomers, pocket watches heavy
in their jeans, whole baskets of longed-for

pulled teeth. A dark savoy, the devil of which
is a tiny thing called age. Here we are. I know.

I'm the warmed wax, and I'm the rag
that's rubbed the table. I'm the one who

pulls the chair for you to sit. Drink. Now
the afternoon pours through the iron-

framed windows, whorl and pulse of heat,
a reef set sail to still and lasso the aching tide.

ICE TONGS

Fall lasted, but there was nothing to slake—the tire,
the iron, the box of kittens in the cupboard

under the stairs. Your knitting, your basket, your
beard a vine and vined to mine. Nothing here

to slake at all, move on. Leave me to my lost wallet
and damp towel, leave me to those kittens.

My bargain is that you leave me everything: Mario
and Luigi and the princess, hay loft and BMX track,

artichoke and beet, snow and ice and storm and hail.
I eat your marginalia, I play your ax, I water your orchard

and fill my baskets with your gloveless, handless, too-warm
October harvest. You ruined me. Happen again, little book.

V

OLIVE PITTER

I imagine you apricot, so.
All of you. Honeyed and snug
in the pit of time since time
began. I imagine you anchored
within my small ocean, waiting,
disregarding all attempts
at swaying your seed selves.

Whatever keeps you there,
remember. All the months lost
to strung-up nights, all the callous
time remember: you are mine—
the weight of small birds
bore you up in midsummer dawn.

SIFTER

Child that wasn't, everyday. Child
that set the wide skillet of my mind
to humming. Child that wasn't, again.

Morning arrives like a tug
and anchors in the shoal—mud,
muck, suck, spray, take, take

the boots off my feet. Anybody's
guess. So this is a month: coffee
capped with cream, the bulging

honeycomb of the ribs; January;
I pick through the lentils by hand
and I am ruthless for perfection.

JAM FUNNEL

Thinking you could hold court even in this belly. You
who do not exist: once it seemed the function of poetry

was to *mean*. It was to last and to be and to hold
a place for you. While I slept you stood in the kitchen

watching beans soak in the silver bowl.
These messy omens and symbols and how,

like Odysseus, we might get home after all.
Stiff filler, you were an epoch in

our bed. Thinking you could divide your cells
even now. I spared nothing for you.

MISCHIEF

Also, summer lasted. We flung our bodies on the bed,
I slept with ice packs wrapped to my chest,

heat pulsed through the walls, & we whispered through
the fans' motors. Such mangoes en flambé we'd meant to mark

this summer excruciating. And then, tonight, so tipping
in our chairs, at last, so chilled, so shutting windows in a flurry,

you heaved your weight against the sills. We aren't
in our bodies these days. All those babies in my head

were never real. I was there. Their tiny bodies dropped.
In summer, heat pools even in the iron tub & spouts.

COLANDER

Berry box full of foxes, I breathe milk.
I stand tall for hours and frighten an egg
that won't crack with my fiery stare.

Go, I say. Now. He who hesitates is lost.
My foxes are your shadows' shadows—
and their tails ache with holding your shape.

So go. Leave this oven. I breathe milk.
I am the size of a pea—and I wash my feet.
I drive trucks. I am foxes.

I wish the stars right out of the sky.
I squint. Patience, patience, patience. I foul
and fillet and filly and fool—for you.

SALAD

In your hand,
a lemon half;
your other hand
held the reamer. I

let the knife hang
midair and drip.
Seeds, coarse-cut
salt, tall glasses—

all my faults
come down to
impatience. A thin
mesh sieve is all

that keeps me
in this kitchen.
That's not true.
Pomegranate,

the fontanel bones
of a skull, as yet,
still seed. Fathomless
want, core, pit.

EARLY, EARLY

My earl, my earl of grey, my grey goose, my foie gras,
we swam under the dock on the hottest day of the summer

and twined our ankles to the lake grass and printed our names
with our wet fingers on the wholly impermanent underside

of the sinking planks. And I wrote yours and the turtles weren't
biting and the fish stayed away and the wind carried the voices of

two old men in their boat to our ears. Whatever forgiveness
you're seeking, I give it. Marigold lank in the heat of what's only

getting hotter; the cats wild with lethargy; their bowls untouched
and water gone dry—what can I give you but a chilled noon bowl of anything.

VALENTINE

Even in her wildest fancies the ocean had never been so huge.
-Halldor Laxness, *Independent People*

Even at dawn while your breath simmers
that low boil and parses the steam into a stippled

ranging lost fleet bound for an unseen coast,
even as the sun edges its heaving belly

over the ridge and the cat sits on the vent,
waiting for the heat to click on. Even as my mind

goes monochromatic: banana, banana, toast, peanut
butter, and the neighbor closes his car door

and starts his engine. Even, achingly, at dawn
while I wonder at this great luck—to be here,

with you, in the chill room, while the planet heats
and it is still the night before what is yet to be,

and even at dawn with our feet hummocked
in the flannel while grouse in some distant fen

wander in and out of the low mist where the ground
is bare of turf, growing brighter, even then.

CODDLING CUP

There would be a shoeblack

in debt up to his ears,
with a wife and seven children

even in the 80s

for lack of a better analogy.
There would be a woodpile

two cords deep under the eaves

with mouse nests snug between
the split apple trunk.

On the shelf next to this coddling cup,

where everything is found,
there would be a porcelain plate

with three little bears for a baby

named—. There would be a sigh
for—. There would be a wool

hat and mittens on a string for—.

And in our wish for her new
new year, we'd wish for more.

ACKNOWLEDGMENTS

I gratefully acknowledge the journals and anthologies in which these poems first appeared (sometimes with different titles):

32 Poems: "Cleaver," "Churchkey," and "Coddling Cup"
42opus: "There is no mystery"
AGNI (online): "Refusal" and "Egg Topper"
Beloit Poetry Journal: "Bread Knife" and "Jam Funnel"
Blackbird: "(The world is my) Oyster," "Burning" "Mischief"
Cincinnati Review: "Saucer" and "Sifter"
Connotation Press: "Trivet," "Reamer," and "Ramekin"
Cream City Review: "Linen"
Ecotone: "Olive Pitter" and "Ice Pick"
FIELD: "Singing It" and "Jar"
Gastronomica: "Double Boiler," "French Press," and "Pasta Pin"
Guernica: "Everything"
Hayden's Ferry Review: "Spoon"
Kenyon Review: "Canary" and "Pie Bird"
Ninth Letter: "Bowl"
Ploughshares: "Poem"
Prairie Schooner: "Pepper" and "It's all"
Poetry Northwest: "Pear" and "If the mind"
Quarterly West: "Feast"
Superstition Review: "Mortar and Pestle," "Ladle," "Spoon Rest," "Rolling Pin," and "Whisk"
Sycamore Review: "Then" and "Apron"
Whitman Cooks (anthology): "Double Boiler" and "9 x 13 Inch Baking Dish"

I am also very grateful for the MacDowell Colony whose generous assistance supported the making of these poems.

The New Southern Voices Book Prize was established in 2013 and is a biennual prize awarded to an emerging Southern poet who has published at most one previous collection of poetry. It is awarded for a book-length collection of poems written originally in English.

HUB CITY
PRESS

HUB CITY PRESS is a non-profit independent press in Spartanburg, SC that publishes well-crafted, high-quality works by new and established authors, with an emphasis on the Southern experience. We are committed to high-caliber novels, short stories, poetry, plays, memoir, and works emphasizing regional culture and history. We are particularly interested in books with a strong sense of place.

Hub City Press is an imprint of the non-profit Hub City Writers Project, founded in 1995 to foster a sense of community through the literary arts. Our metaphor of organization purposely looks backward to the nineteenth century when Spartanburg was known as the "hub city," a place where railroads converged and departed.